Original title:
Walls of Wonder

Copyright © 2024 Creative Arts Management OÜ
All rights reserved.

Author: Tim Wood
ISBN HARDBACK: 978-9916-88-078-4
ISBN PAPERBACK: 978-9916-88-079-1

Labyrinthine Landscapes of Thought

Winding paths of silent minds,
Twists and turns, no guide to find.
Echoes whisper through the haze,
In the depths, a quiet maze.

Figures dance in fleeting light,
Shadows play from day to night.
A search for truth beneath the veil,
In this land, the spirits sail.

Fables etching the Edges

Stories written in the stars,
Tales of old, of war and scars.
Each word a brush, each line a thread,
Crafting worlds where dreams are fed.

Wisdom whispers from the past,
Lessons learned, forever cast.
In the margins, life's deep lore,
Fables open every door.

Hidden Corners of the World

Secret paths behind the trees,
Wonders wait on softest breeze.
Caves of mystery, shadows play,
In the heart where echoes stay.

A lantern glows in dusky light,
Shining bright through endless night.
Adventure calls from every stone,
In these corners, we are home.

Reflections in the Room of Dreams

Mirrors catch the thoughts that fly,
Silhouettes of dreams gone by.
Whispers float like clouds of silk,
Cradled gently, warmth of milk.

Timeless moments stay in frames,
Each reflection hides our names.
In this space, we laugh, we weep,
Where the waking world is deep.

Shadows of the Hidden Realm

In twilight whispers, secrets dwell,
Where shadows weave a distant spell.
Beneath the trees where silence sighs,
A world awaits, where magic lies.

Echoes of laughter, faint and low,
Dance on the breeze, where shadows flow.
Mysteries wrapped in twilight's hue,
In the hidden realm, all feels new.

Boundaries of Dreams Unspoken

In night's embrace, our visions soar,
Beyond the limits of reality's door.
Gentle wisps of hope take flight,
Guided softly by the moonlight.

Silent wishes in the air,
Whispered moments, we boldly dare.
In this space where dreams collide,
Unspoken truths, we cannot hide.

Lattice of Lost Treasures

In dusty chests, the memories lie,
Of laughter shared, of days gone by.
Each trinket tells a tale anew,
Of love and loss, of skies so blue.

Beneath the surface, stories dwell,
In woven patterns, they cast a spell.
Diligent hearts search through the past,
In the lattice, treasures held fast.

The Fortress of Forgotten Tales

Amidst the stones, old stories sigh,
Heroes and myths, they never die.
Echoes linger in the air,
Whispers of battles, tales we share.

Time's embrace wraps all around,
In this fortress, lost is found.
Each creak and moan, a voice from yore,
In the heart of history, we explore.

Ghosts of Memories inscribed in Brick

Whispers linger 'neath the stone,
Etched in silence, all alone.
Each crack a tale, each shadow deep,
A history lost, a secret we keep.

Time stands still in the dampened air,
Haunting echoes, love and despair.
Ghostly figures dance in the light,
Remnants of laughter, fading from sight.

In the corners, stories weave,
Of dreams once held, and hearts that grieve.
Brick by brick, the past unfolds,
A tapestry of lives once bold.

Beneath the surface, spirits sigh,
Beneath the weight, they seem to fly.
Memories bloom where shadows meet,
Ghosts of the past, in brick, retreat.

Echoes of Enchantment

In forests deep where whispers tread,
Magic lingers, lightly spread.
Crystal streams and moonlit glades,
Nature's songs in twilight fades.

Stars awaken, softly glow,
Shimmering echoes, tales bestow.
Winds caress the ancient trees,
Lifting voices on the breeze.

Enchantments dance in silver night,
Flickering flames, a soft delight.
The night reveals its wondrous charms,
Holding tight with sacred arms.

Lost in dreams and starlit plays,
We find ourselves in twilight's maze.
Echoes singing, sweet and clear,
Enchantment calls, forever near.

Fortresses of Dreams

Within the walls of thought and hope,
Castles rise, a sturdy slope.
Each brick a wish, a silent plea,
Fortresses built for you and me.

Clouds may darken skies above,
Yet dreams endure, a tale of love.
In every heart, a kingdom waits,
A realm where fate and chance creates.

Through stormy nights and radiant days,
Imagine paths where courage plays.
Strong as mountains, soft as streams,
We defend our world of dreams.

With every heartbeat, every stare,
These fortresses stand strong and rare.
In our minds, they bloom and thrive,
Fortresses of dreams, forever alive.

Veils of Illusion

Gossamer threads that twist and weave,
A fragile dance, we dare believe.
Hidden truths behind the smile,
Veils of illusion, beguile awhile.

Mirrors reflect what eyes can't see,
Shadows whisper, setting free.
In the depths where secrets lie,
Veils conceal the reasons why.

Ephemeral moments pass with grace,
Finding solace in a disguise.
What is real, and what's a game?
Veils of illusion, none the same.

As the dawn begins to break,
Layers peel, and hearts awake.
In this world of blurred lines spun,
Veils of illusion, we are one.

The Gilded Limits

In gilded frames we find our place,
The whispers caught in velvet space.
A path adorned with dreams so sweet,
Yet shadows dance beneath our feet.

We chase the gold, the fleeting light,
While hidden truths escape our sight.
The boundaries drawn in golden thread,
Yet in those lines, our hopes are wed.

With every step, the weight we bear,
A fragile heart laid partially bare.
Yet in the gilded, we still yearn,
For freedom's song, our spirits burn.

The limits fade, we break away,
Embrace the dusk, embrace the sway.
Beyond the gold, our journey waits,
To find the truth that liberates.

The Symphony of Silence

In silence' grasp, a world unfolds,
Where whispers weave through dreams retold.
The notes of quiet fill the air,
A symphony beyond compare.

Each pause a canvas, pure and wide,
Where thoughts can drift and freely glide.
The heartbeats echo, soft and low,
A rhythm only few might know.

In shadows cast by moonlit glow,
The silence hums, a sacred flow.
A dance of minds, an inner tune,
That twirls along with silver moon.

Embrace the hush, let worries cease,
Find harmony and sweet release.
In silence lies a world profound,
A symphony in every sound.

Tapestries of Time

In threads of gold, the stories weave,
Tapestries that we believe.
Each moment stitched with love and care,
A canvas rich, forever rare.

The hands of time will pull and twist,
In patterns that we can't resist.
From dawn's first light to twilight's fall,
Every thread speaks, it knows it all.

With every year a color blends,
And every joy and sorrow sends.
A dance of fate in vibrant hues,
The tales of life, the paths we choose.

So let the needle guide your thread,
In tapestries where dreams are spread.
The fabric of our lives will show,
A legacy in time will grow.

Spheres of Serenity

In the hush of twilight's glow,
Soft whispers of the wind do flow.
Gentle shadows dance on trees,
A tranquil heart finds its ease.

Beneath the stars, the world stands still,
Moonlight bathes the silent hill.
Each breath a balm, each thought a prayer,
In this moment, peace lays bare.

Rippling streams through meadows weave,
In nature's arms, we learn to believe.
In the calm, our spirits soar,
Spheres of serenity, evermore.

Kaleidoscopic Keep

Colors swirl in playful light,
Shapes and shadows glide in flight.
A canvas born from dreams awake,
Endless patterns, reality to shake.

Windows framed with hues divine,
Each glance reveals a new design.
Mirrored truths in vibrant scenes,
Where imagination reigns, it gleans.

In this keep of wonders bright,
Chasing visions, pure delight.
From heart to mind, let spirit leap,
Kaleidoscopic keep, ours to keep.

The Silent Citadel

In the heart of the ancient stone,
Whispers linger, though alone.
Echoes of a time now past,
In this fortress, memories cast.

Walls stand sturdy, dreams entombed,
In shadowed halls where legends bloomed.
The silent citadel, proud and grand,
Shelters secrets, lost yet planned.

Through each corridor, tales unfold,
Of courage, honor, hearts of gold.
In stillness, stories weave their thread,
Embracing all who've come and fled.

Prism of Possibilities

A ray of light through crystal breaks,
A spectrum born, each moment shakes.
In every hue, a chance to see,
The paths we take, our destiny.

With every choice, a color blooms,
Filling hearts, dispelling glooms.
In the canvas of the soul's delight,
Endless dreams take flight, ignite.

Through life's prism, visions dance,
Infinite roads in a fleeting glance.
With courage held and hearts set free,
We embrace the vast, the mystery.

Secrets of the Stone

Whispers echo through the night,
A granite heart holds tales of light.
Beneath the surface, stories lie,
In silence, ancient secrets sigh.

Time has carved its gentle mark,
In shadows deep, we hear the spark.
Each crack and fissure, a voice now weak,
In rugged beauty, the stones still speak.

Through ages passed, they watch and wait,
Guardians of past, lovers of fate.
Their quiet wisdom, a guiding hand,
In every crevice, we understand.

With every step, we tread with care,
In the stillness, a truth laid bare.
Unravel then the tales untold,
In the secrets of the stone, behold.

Canvases of Color

Brush of sunrise paints the sky,
Every hue a soft goodbye.
Morning whispers in vibrant tones,
Nature's palette, all its owns.

Fields bloom bright with every shade,
Dancing colors, dreams invade.
Roses blush and violets sigh,
In the canvas, love can fly.

Strokes of laughter grace the air,
Crimson joys and midnight stare.
In the twilight, shadows blend,
Artful moments never end.

From every corner, beauty flows,
A masterpiece that gently grows.
In every color, life is seen,
A vibrant symphony, serene.

Gates to the Unknown

Hidden portals, shadows cast,
Whispers of the future and the past.
Glimmers beckon through the night,
Curiosity ignites the light.

Each threshold holds a chance to see,
A world beyond, wild and free.
Mystery dances in the air,
Inviting hearts, prepared to dare.

Winds of change and paths untried,
With open minds, we turn the tide.
Beyond the gate, the journey grows,
Through every door, a secret flows.

Tread softly on this sacred ground,
In every silence, truth resounds.
Gates to the unknown timely chime,
Embrace the journey, step through time.

Embrace of Enchantment

In the twilight's gentle glow,
Whispers weave where fairies go.
Magic lingers in the air,
In every heart, a dream to share.

Moonlight dances on the stream,
Fading softly, like a dream.
Enchanted woods, a spell is cast,
In every moment, shadows past.

Laughter echoes through the trees,
Carried softly by the breeze.
Mystic wonders intertwine,
In this embrace, our souls align.

Hold the magic, feel the night,
In the darkness, find the light.
Where dreams awaken and spirits soar,
In the embrace of enchantment, forevermore.

The Silent Symphony

In stillness blooms a sound,
A whisper lost, not found.
Notes float on the breeze,
Soft echoes in the trees.

A melody of the night,
Stars twinkle, pure delight.
Moonlight strums the air,
Creating tunes, rare and fair.

Silence holds the heart's tune,
Crickets chirp, sing to the moon.
Harmony in shade,
A tranquil serenade.

In shadows, music flows,
Where no one else goes.
Each breath a quiet song,
In this space, we belong.

The Chromatic Cloister

Colors dance in gentle light,
A canvas woven bright.
Each hue, a sacred place,
Where shadows find their grace.

Violet whispers warm and true,
Emerald dreams rush through.
Crimson echoes fill the air,
In gardens beyond compare.

Golden rays of morning flow,
Behind the walls, secrets grow.
Azure skies above us bend,
In color, we transcend.

A sacred bond, a vivid sphere,
Where every shade draws near.
In the cloister's sweet embrace,
We honor every space.

Obscured Pathways

In fading light, the trails unwind,
Lost secrets of the mind.
Twists and turns, a hidden way,
Whispers beckon, come and play.

Footsteps fade on ancient ground,
In the stillness, truths are found.
Overgrown with tangled vines,
The heart of nature intertwines.

Misty fog, a shroud of gray,
Guiding souls who drift astray.
Through the maze, a gentle pull,
In the shadows, life is full.

Beyond the thorns, a light shall gleam,
Awaking every dream.
For in the dark, the path is clear,
Obscured treasures, drawing near.

Enchanted Enclosures

Within the walls of emerald shade,
A world of wonders, gently laid.
Sunlight dapples on the floor,
Inviting hearts to seek for more.

Within the whispers of the breeze,
Nature sings with playful ease.
Petals dance in fragrant air,
Each breath—a moment rare.

Glimmers shimmer on the skin,
A magic that draws us in.
In corners where fairies play,
Imagination finds its way.

With every step, the spirit flows,
In this haven, beauty grows.
Enclosed in dreams, hearts shall reign,
In enchanted joy, we remain.

The Boundless Canvas

With every stroke the colors blend,
A world awaits with tales to send.
Dreams drift softly on the breeze,
In whispers shared beneath the trees.

A dash of blue, a hint of gold,
An endless scene, a sight to behold.
Each hue a secret, bold and bright,
In this vast space of pure delight.

The artists' hands, they weave and dance,
Transforming thoughts into romance.
Stars twinkle down with gentle grace,
Upon this grand, uncharted space.

In every corner, stories lie,
A boundless canvas stretching high.
Where silence speaks in vibrant tones,
And beauty whispers from the bones.

Gateways of Mystery

In shadows deep, the secrets hide,
Behind the walls, the echoes bide.
Ancient paths that twist and turn,
In every glance, the spark will burn.

The mist unveils, the night ignites,
With every step, the heart ignites.
Through silent doors, our souls will roam,
Exploring realms that feel like home.

A flicker glows in distant lands,
As whispers weave with gentle hands.
The journey calls with velvet voice,
In every shadow, we rejoice.

What lies beyond these veils of night?
A world unknown, yet filled with light.
With courage fierce, we dare to seek,
The gateways vast, we shall not sneak.

Silhouettes of Saga

As twilight falls, the stories rise,
In silhouettes against the skies.
Figures dance in soft twilight,
Tales of old take wing in flight.

Elders speak of days long past,
Their words a spell, a shadow cast.
With every tale, a heart aglow,
In quiet realms where legends flow.

The moonlit path reflects the lore,
Each step unveils the tales of yore.
An echo here, a sigh of fate,
Silhouettes weave, our hopes await.

In whispers soft, the sagas blend,
With every dusk, the journey bends.
A tapestry of dreams and night,
In silhouettes, the past takes flight.

Mosaic of Marvels

Each piece a story, bright and bold,
In every shade, a memory told.
Fragments scattered, yet aligned,
A work of art, love intertwined.

From darkest nights to sunlit days,
The colors shift in wondrous ways.
With every touch, a heart will soar,
In every glance, a new explore.

The whispers blend, the tales ignite,
A mosaic formed in radiant light.
In harmony, our spirits rise,
United here beneath the skies.

This canvas made of dreams and time,
In every piece, a perfect rhyme.
The marvels dwell, a sight to see,
In every heart, a tapestry.

The Veiled Mirage

In the heat of the day, it glimmers bright,
A phantom of hope, just out of sight.
Waves of illusion, they dance and tease,
Promising treasures beneath the trees.

But closer we draw, the shimmer fades,
Revealing the truth where magic wades.
A world so vibrant, yet hiding its heart,
In the veil of the mirage, we each play our part.

Beneath the surface, reality waits,
With open arms at the shimmering gates.
What we seek often lingers near,
In the essence of dreams, we hold so dear.

Through the layers, we wander and roam,
In the veiled mirage, we find our home.

Dimensions of Delight

In colors that sparkle, joy takes flight,
Each moment a canvas, pure and bright.
Dimensions unfold with every embrace,
We dance through the spaces, a joyous chase.

Laughter echoes in shadows and light,
Where dreams intertwine, a magical sight.
With every heartbeat, a new story grows,
In dimensions of delight, the spirit glows.

Time bends and sways, a playful thread,
Connecting our hearts as we laugh and tread.
Beyond the horizon, where wonders resound,
In the depths of delight, true joy is found.

Let the world spin in hues of your choice,
Invite the magic, let your heart rejoice.
In this tapestry woven, we create our fate,
In dimensions of delight, we celebrate.

Arches of Awe

Beneath vast skies, the arches soar,
Whispers of legends, tales of yore.
Nature's grandeur, a stunning display,
In the boldness of forms, we find our way.

Every step taken, the earth sings true,
Under the arches, old meets the new.
A bridge to the heavens, a gateway of dreams,
In silence and beauty, the heart softly gleams.

The shadows they cast, a dance of grace,
In each golden moment, we find our place.
Through arches of awe, we discover the light,
Illuminating paths in the depth of the night.

Let your spirit wander, let your heart soar,
In the embrace of the arches, seek evermore.
In the echoes of wonder, life finds its call,
Within the arches of awe, we're part of it all.

The Shadowed Frames

In corners of rooms where silence lingers,
Stories reside, in the dust of fingers.
Frames hold the past in their faded embrace,
Each artifact whispers of time and place.

Within shadowed frames, memories glow,
Tales of laughter and tears, ebb and flow.
Images captured in moments so sweet,
Within each reflection, the heart skips a beat.

From portraits to landscapes, life's essence shines,
In the echo of ages, where history aligns.
Each frame a window, a glimpse into years,
In shadowed frames live our hopes and fears.

So gather the memories, let them be known,
In the shadowed frames, we are never alone.
In the tapestry woven, our stories reclaim,
Life through the lens, in the shadowed frame.

Citadels of Curiosity

Within the walls of thought, we roam,
Questions echo, seeking home.
Each answer hides a tale untold,
In shadows deep, wisdom unfolds.

A whispered breeze through ancient halls,
Invites the mind where stillness calls.
Each doorway opens to the vast,
Unlocking futures, freeing pasts.

Beneath the arch of seeking eyes,
The heart aspires, the spirit flies.
In every turn, a spark ignites,
Illuminating endless sights.

Curiosity, a noble steed,
Across the landscape it will lead.
In citadels where dreams take flight,
We delve for truth, we chase the light.

The Art of Restraint

In stillness lies a quiet grace,
The world rushes, a frenetic race.
Yet in the pause, the power gleams,
Like gentle waters, reflecting dreams.

To hold the reins, to know the time,
A measured step, a silent rhyme.
In every breath, control we find,
A masterpiece of heart and mind.

With patience woven into each thread,
Restraint speaks softly, where words have fled.
It guides the art of making space,
For thoughts to blossom, for fears to brace.

From chaos blooms a quiet soul,
Embracing calm, we become whole.
In life's great dance, learn to refrain,
The art of restraint, a soft refrain.

Beyond the Fences

Where fences mark the line of fear,
A whispered call, the wild draws near.
Beyond the bounds, the heart begins,
To seek the place where freedom wins.

With every leap, a daring chance,
To lose the chains, to join the dance.
In open fields, the spirit flies,
Awake to truths, beneath the skies.

The colors blend, the horizons shift,
In endless space, our souls can drift.
No longer caged by walls or sound,
In nature's arms, a peace is found.

So step outside, embrace the thrill,
Beyond the fences, feel the chill.
For life awaits on the other side,
A journey wide, a heart open wide.

Towers of Intrigue

In castles tall, the stories brew,
A labyrinth where shadows grew.
With secrets draped in cloaks of night,
The air is thick with whispered fright.

Each turret holds a mystery tight,
Guarded whispers in fading light.
Who walked these halls, who played their part,
With blood and tears, with flame and heart?

Beyond the ramparts, tales entwine,
A tapestry of fate divine.
The echoes linger, casting spells,
In every corner, a story dwells.

With quests that pull the brave and bold,
The towers stand, both fierce and old.
In realms where intrigue weaves its web,
The heart and mind must take their ebb.

The Arcane Enclave

In shadowed halls where whispers dwell,
Secrets held in muted spell.
Ancient tomes on shelves align,
Guarded truths in inked design.

Cloaked figures drift through twilight dim,
Their faces lost, their destinies grim.
A flicker of light from crystal bright,
Illuminates paths concealed from sight.

Echoes of chants from ages long,
Resonate gently like an ancient song.
Winds of wisdom breathe through the air,
Encircling all in a somber prayer.

In the heart of this arcane ground,
The pulse of magic softly resounds.
Here, time holds still, the world fades away,
In the enclave where shadows play.

The Enchanted Refuge

Beneath the boughs of weeping trees,
Whispers dance upon the breeze.
A sanctuary for the lost,
Where seekers find the wonders tossed.

Mossy stones that cradle dreams,
Reflecting light in silver streams.
In this refuge, hearts can mend,
And weary souls find a true friend.

Flowers bloom with colors rare,
Filling the space with fragrant air.
The melody of nature sings,
Drawing forth the joy it brings.

Here, time drifts like a gentle sigh,
Underneath the endless sky.
An enchanted haven, pure and bright,
A beacon in the soft twilight.

Spirals of Solitude

In the quiet corners of a mind,
Spirals twist, a path unkind.
Thoughts like shadows loom and sway,
Guiding dreams that slip away.

Whispers echo in hollow halls,
Where the weight of silence falls.
Lonely stars blink in the night,
Fleeting visions, lost from sight.

Yet in this solitude, a spark,
Illuminates the deepening dark.
A dance of shadows, a silent trance,
Inviting the heart to take a chance.

Embrace the stillness, the haunting calls,
Find solace as the spirit sprawls.
In spirals of solitude, we grow,
Learning from the ebb and flow.

Pavilions of the Past

In distant lands where echoes play,
Pavilions rise, a grand ballet.
Stories etched in weathered stone,
Whisper histories, overgrown.

Each arch and beam holds memories tight,
Of laughter soft and shadows bright.
Through corridors of days gone by,
The ghosts of time linger and sigh.

Sunlight filters through the leaves,
Casting patterns, as the heart believes.
Every step a journey vast,
In pavilions where spells are cast.

So wander these halls, let the past embrace,
The dance of time in a sacred space.
For in the stories, we find our way,
In the pavilions of yesterday.

Silhouettes Beneath the Surface

In twilight's hush, shadows dance,
Beneath the waves, a fleeting glance.
Whispers linger, secrets play,
Silhouettes drift, then fade away.

Ghostly figures in the deep,
Where moonlit beams and currents sweep.
Veils of water, dreams entwine,
In silent depths, the worlds align.

Echoes ripple, stories untold,
Ancient tales of love and gold.
In the stillness, hearts confined,
Silhouettes lost, never defined.

Time stands still, yet never waits,
The ocean's mouth, it softly relates.
Beneath the surface, life persists,
In quiet shadows, we coexist.

Echoes of Enchantment

In forest glades where fairies sing,
The night blooms forth with jeweled wing.
Whispers wrap around the trees,
Echoes linger, carried by the breeze.

Underneath the starlit skies,
Magic swirls in tired sighs.
Moonlit paths draw us near,
Every shadow holds a cheer.

Wandering souls on paths of gold,
Seeking dreams that dare unfold.
In the twilight's gentle embrace,
We find the light in each soft place.

Through the veil of time we roam,
In every heart, we find our home.
Echoes of enchantment tease,
A world of wonder, hearts at ease.

The Unseen Architecture of Magic

In shadows deep, where dreams align,
A structure built of thread and twine.
Invisible hands weave with care,
Fortresses rise from whispered air.

Cascading light through hidden seams,
An artistry of shape and dreams.
Twists of fate and paths unknown,
In silent chambers, seeds are sown.

Ancient codes in every stone,
A blueprint etched, yet still alone.
Where logic falters, magic thrives,
In the unseen, true life derives.

Layers fold and secrets sway,
In every nook, the mystics play.
The unseen art we long to know,
In magic's heart, the soul will grow.

Veils of Intrigue and Imagination

Behind the curtain, stories hide,
Veils of intrigue, ever tied.
Imagination paints the scene,
In colors rich, bold, and serene.

Figures loom in hazy dream,
Crafting worlds, or so it seems.
A flicker here, a shimmer there,
Mysteries dance on gentle air.

Every glance, a secret shared,
In whispered tones, our hearts laid bare.
Veils entwine, revealing grace,
In shadows cast, we find our place.

The mind constructs a wondrous maze,
Where fantasy intertwines with rays.
In veils of intrigue, we shall find,
The art of dreams, forever entwined.

The Cloisters of Curious Spirits

In shadows deep where whispers dwell,
Curious spirits weave their spell.
Through arches old, the echoes roam,
In cloisters dark, they find their home.

Flickering lights, a dance of fate,
Stories linger, resonate.
With every sigh, the past ignites,
In vaulted halls, lost souls take flight.

Gentle winds through ancient stone,
Awaken tales of those we've known.
In twilight's grace, the secrets gleam,
In quietude, we share the dream.

Come wander here, let silence guide,
The curious spirits, forever side.
In cloisters vast, let heart's refrain,
Bring forth the joy, the love, the pain.

Tapestries of Timeworn Secrets

Thread by thread, the stories bind,
In timeworn tapestries, lost yet kind.
Patterns weave through hands of fate,
Each stitch holds memories innate.

Colors faded, yet vibrant still,
Whispers echo, a tender thrill.
In woven warmth, our lives align,
Unraveling dreams, sweet and divine.

Guarded tales of love and strife,
Adorned in fabric, a tapestry of life.
In intricate knots, old secrets dwell,
With every glance, a silent spell.

Gaze upon these threads of yore,
As time unveils what was before.
In every fold, a piece of heart,
In tapestries, our souls impart.

The Enigma of Enclosed Spaces

Beneath the roof, the walls confine,
An enigma wrapped in design.
With every corner, shadows play,
In closed confines, the mind will stray.

Windows small, yet visions grand,
A universe in a grain of sand.
Hidden depths in silence bloom,
Within these walls, we chase the room.

The whispers linger, thoughts conceal,
In enclosed spaces, time can heal.
With careful steps, we seek the truth,
In spaces tight, we find our youth.

Every cranny holds a tale,
Of hopes and fears, in dreams we sail.
An enigma vast, yet snugly penned,
In closed embrace, our hearts transcend.

Riddles Wrapped in Earth and Stone

In caverns deep, where shadows blend,
Riddles wrapped the earth does send.
With each stone turned, a question grows,
In silence thick, the mystery flows.

Roots entwined in ancient lore,
The whispers call from times of yore.
Beneath the ground, where secrets sleep,
In riddles cast, the watchers peep.

Echoes murmur, forgotten trails,
In rocky halls where silence pales.
Each grain of sand, a story spun,
In earth and stone, the journey's begun.

Through labyrinths carved in nature's art,
Riddles unfold, a quest to start.
In every twist, a heart awaits,
Wrapped in earth, where destiny creates.

Boundless Facades

In a world of painted dreams,
Where shadows dance and shimmer,
Lies a truth behind the seams,
A facade that feels much dimmer.

Gaze upon the gilded hue,
The smiles that mask the sorrow,
What's hidden might frighten you,
Yet hope dares to face tomorrow.

Echoed laughter fills the air,
Yet whispers murmur low,
Each phase holds a hidden glare,
In the boundless ebb and flow.

Still, beneath the painted guise,
A vibrant heart beats strong,
To break the veils and find the prize,
Where truth and love belong.

Canopies of Captivation

Beneath the emerald leaves so high,
A tapestry of dreams is spun,
Where melodies of laughter lie,
In warm embrace of golden sun.

Each whisper flows through branches wide,
A serenade of nature's song,
Entwined within, we lose our pride,
As time weaves fleeting moments long.

Birds will join in sweet delight,
Their voices echo, soft and clear,
In canopies where hearts take flight,
A dance of joy that draws us near.

In every shade, in every breeze,
A touch of magic lingers on,
In shades of green, we find our ease,
A world reborn with every dawn.

The Secret Garden Gate

A gate of rust and ivy twines,
Hides whispers of forgotten lore,
Beyond, a realm of olden signs,
Where flowers bloom forevermore.

In shadows deep, the fragrance calls,
A promise of what waits in dreams,
With each step, soft beauty sprawls,
In moonlight's glow, the starlight beams.

Petals brush against the skin,
While secrets linger in the air,
Awakened dreams begin to spin,
In silence, thoughts begin to flare.

As twilight paints the world in gold,
The gate stands firm, a timeless guide,
In memories both new and old,
Where hope and wonder shall abide.

Whispering Divides

Between the lines where silence breathes,
A distance deeper than the sea,
In tangled thoughts that love bequeathes,
A bridge built from uncertainty.

Yet in the gaps, a spark ignites,
A lingering touch, a glance, a sigh,
Where longing speaks in softest nights,
And hearts collide without a why.

Through gentle winds, the yearning flows,
As time escapes on fragile wings,
In every space, the longing grows,
Uniting souls in whispered strings.

So let the divides turn to embrace,
For love knows not the weight of fear,
In tender moments, hearts will trace,
The beauty found when you are near.

The Artful Abyss

In shadows deep, where whispers play,
Colors swirl in a muted ballet.
Each stroke a story, each hue a sigh,
An ocean of dreams where lost thoughts lie.

Canvas stretched, the heart exposed,
Emotions tangled, vividly enclosed.
In this abyss, the soul takes flight,
Crafting secrets in the dead of night.

Every brush an echo, every shade a call,
A dance of shadows that flickers and falls.
Art becomes the voice of the unseen,
In the depths of beauty, we glean.

With every layer, new truths unfold,
Stories of warmth, or bitterly cold.
In this artful abyss, we dare to create,
A world in colors, rich and ornate.

Veils of Veneration

Whispers of reverence in the dusky light,
Spirits of ages, cloaked in the night.
Each veil a story, each fold a prayer,
In the temple of shadows, silence hangs in the air.

Through silken drapes, an echoing hum,
Voices of ancestors, softly they come.
In moments of stillness, they guide and inspire,
Lighting the paths that lead to desire.

The air thick with history, sacred and pure,
Memories linger, a fragile allure.
We bow to the whispers, a collective breath,
In these veils of veneration, we dance with death.

With each gentle touch, a story unfurls,
The heart swells with echoes of ancient worlds.
Veils of remembrance, threads finely spun,
Binding our souls till the journey is done.

Citadel of Secrets

Walls of stone, carved with time,
Echoes of laughter, the sweet chime.
Shadows dance through corridors wide,
Guarding the mysteries they quietly hide.

In every chamber, a whispering tale,
Shrouded in silence, where dreams might sail.
A heart beats within, a measured sound,
In the citadel's depths, wonders abound.

The tapestry woven with threads of fate,
Each secret kept, a passion innate.
Beneath the arches, the past remains,
In layers of dust, history reigns.

As twilight falls, the stories awaken,
In shadows stirred, the unspoken shaken.
Here lies the heart, the essence unbound,
In this citadel, true treasure is found.

Frameworks of Fantasy

In realms of imagination, dreams take flight,
Crafted with care, in the soft twilight.
Through portals of wonder, we wander and weave,
In frameworks of fantasy, we dare to believe.

Castles in clouds, floating on high,
Dragons and fairies, painting the sky.
With each turn of thought, a new world appears,
Bridging the gaps with laughter and tears.

The quill dances freely, ink spills like gold,
Stories of magic, waiting to be told.
Each word a treasure, each sentence a key,
Unlocking the wonders that dwell in the sea.

In this tapestry woven with threads of delight,
Each stitch holds a promise, a glimmer of light.
In frameworks of fantasy, we sketch our own fate,
A journey of spirit, where dreams resonate.

Sanctuaries of Silent Stories

In quiet halls where whispers dwell,
Ancient tales begin to swell.
The dust of time wraps every word,
In shadows lost, their voices heard.

Beneath the arch of faded light,
Each corner holds a flickering sight.
Through cracks of age, the secrets seep,
A gentle call that stirs the deep.

The silence weaves a tender thread,
Binding spirits of the dead.
Their laughter echoes, soft and slow,
In sanctuaries where dreams still flow.

Against the walls, the memories rise,
A tapestry of whispered sighs.
In reverie, they dance and spin,
As silent stories weave within.

The Enclosure of Endless Possibilities

Behind the gate of dreams untold,
A world unfolds, both brave and bold.
With every step, a tale begins,
In the heart where hope still spins.

A canvas wide, with colors bright,
Infinite paths emerge from light.
In shadows danced, the chances play,
With fate entwined, they find their way.

The breath of life, a whispered breeze,
Invites the heart to roam with ease.
In every corner, wonders gleam,
A labyrinth of thought and dream.

Embrace the unknown, let it unfold,
Unlock the secrets yet untold.
In the enclosure, free your mind,
Endless possibilities you will find.

Echoing Labyrinths of the Heart

In twisting paths where feelings tread,
The heart unfolds with words unsaid.
Through winding turns, a pulse ignites,
In echoes soft, love's flame unites.

Each corridor, a story shared,
Of joy and pain, of being bared.
Amidst the twists, the shadows play,
As memories long gone drift away.

With every echo, secrets bloom,
In gentle light, dispelling gloom.
The heart's own maze, both wild and free,
A tapestry of you and me.

In these labyrinths, we chase the dawn,
Through every turn, we carry on.
For in the echoes, we shall see,
The beauty formed from you and me.

Portals of the Uncharted Mind

In whispered thoughts where visions stir,
The mind reveals, both faint and sure.
Through portals wide, the dreams take flight,
Venturing forth into the night.

With every question, worlds collide,
In realms of wonder, secrets hide.
The boundaries blur, horizons bend,
In this vast space, beginnings end.

A journey deep where shadows play,
In every corner, thoughts lead the way.
Embrace the unknown, let it shine,
The uncharted paths, forever mine.

Between the lines of thought and time,
Ideas dance, in rhythm and rhyme.
Through portals bright, our spirits soar,
In the uncharted mind, we explore.

Paradox of Confined Fantasies

In the corners of my mind, they dwell,
A world of wonders, a silent spell.
Yet trapped within, they cannot fly,
A whispered truth, a muted sigh.

Walls so thick, they cage the light,
Hopes and dreams hide from the sight.
Yet with each thought, they start to bloom,
Confined yet free, they fill the room.

Twilight dances on silent streams,
Echoes of life in vivid dreams.
Paradoxes twist, they intertwine,
In a realm where wishes decline.

Embracing shadows with open hands,
In secret places, the heart understands.
Bound by fears, yet yearn to soar,
A paradox, forevermore.

Mysteries in the Masonry

Old stones whisper secrets of time,
Patterns etched in rhythm and rhyme.
Lost in shadows, stories untold,
Crafted with care, both humble and bold.

Each chisel strike, a tale unfolds,
Of ancient hands, and dreams of gold.
Through cracks and crevices, echoes arise,
A glimpse of the past beneath the skies.

Veils of dust cloak the sacred ground,
In silent corners, the lost are found.
Beneath the arches, histories meet,
With every heartbeat, the stones repeat.

Masonry holds what eyes can't see,
A puzzle graveled in mystery.
In every layer, a world remade,
In every cornerstone, shadows played.

The Citadel of Dreams

Within high towers, where visions gleam,
A fortress stands, woven from dreams.
Its windows glint with secrets bright,
Guarded by hope, veiled in night.

Steps of starlight lead the way,
Through halls where shadows softly sway.
Echoes of laughter, whispers of peace,
In the citadel, heartaches cease.

Walls of silver, roofs of gold,
In this sanctuary, stories unfold.
Time stands still, as fears take flight,
In the citadel, all feels right.

A tapestry of wishes hung high,
Each thread a dream that dares to fly.
Under the moon, where silence seems,
Lives the magic of all our dreams.

Treasures Behind the Threshold

An open door, a hidden space,
Treasures nestled in time's embrace.
Beyond the threshold, wonders gleam,
Whispers of life, a vivid dream.

Forgotten places, shadows cast,
Memories linger, echoes of the past.
With each step, stories unfold,
In corners where the brave once strolled.

Gems of wisdom, relics old,
Held in silence, stories told.
Behind the threshold, the heart takes flight,
In sacred realms, bathed in light.

Exploring depths, where fears dissolve,
In the treasures found, we evolve.
Beyond the door, all truths align,
The journey's end, a sweet design.

Portals of Perception

Through the veil of a whisper, we glide,
Into realms where our thoughts can collide.
Each moment a breath, a chance to explore,
Portals of perception, forevermore.

Colors dance softly, the shadows ignite,
A canvas of dreams in the stillness of night.
With visions that shimmer, they beckon the way,
To mysteries hidden, where secrets play.

In the echo of silence, clarity blooms,
As visions awaken, dispelling the glooms.
We wander through passages, each step a clue,
Portals before us, revealing the new.

Embrace the unknown, let the journey unfold,
In the tapestry woven, bright stories are told.
With every perception, a deeper embrace,
Portals revealing life's vast, wondrous space.

Shimmering Dividers

In the twilight's embrace, softly they gleam,
Shimmering dividers that shimmer and dream.
Between worlds we dance, on the edge of the light,
Boundaries whisper, urging us into the night.

Glistening echoes of stories untold,
Moments of magic in silver and gold.
Each divider a passage, a mark of the way,
To places of wonder, where spirits can play.

Softly they flicker, like stars that align,
Charting the journey through shadows that twine.
In the pulse of the cosmos, connections are made,
Shimmering dividers, where dreams never fade.

From the depths of the heart, to horizons so wide,
Through the shimmering dividers, with hope as our guide.

We walk on the edge, where the worlds intertwine,
Each moment a treasure, each heartbeat divine.

Labyrinths of Light

In the woven paths where shadows take flight,
We wander through labyrinths, glowing with light.
Each twist a new chapter, each turn a surprise,
In the maze of existence, wisdom soon lies.

Glistening corridors beckon us near,
With whispers of secrets that dance on the air.
Lost and yet found, in the flickering glow,
Labyrinths of light, guiding us to go.

Mirrors reflect on the walls of the mind,
A passage of visions, each moment aligned.
In the depths of the labyrinth, courage ignites,
Navigating boldly, amidst all the sights.

Through the heart of the maze, we seek and embrace,
The brilliance of journeys, each moment a grace.
Labyrinths of light lead us to our core,
In the dance of discovery, we crave evermore.

Enigmatic Horizons

Beyond the edge of what we can see,
Enigmatic horizons call out to thee.
In the shades of the dusk, new wonders arise,
Where the earth meets the sky, and dreams crystallize.

With each step we take, the future unfurls,
A tapestry woven in vibrant swirls.
Hidden in twilight, the essence of chance,
Enigmatic horizons invite us to dance.

Through whispers of starlight, we journey afar,
With hope in our hearts, guided by a star.
In the realm of the unknown, we carve out our fate,
Enigmatic horizons, we seek, and we wait.

As day fades to night, and the canvas is clear,
We embrace the mysteries that linger near.
With each new horizon, a promise we find,
In the weave of the cosmos, together, aligned.

Auras of the Unseen

Whispers of light dance in the air,
Colors that shimmer, visions laid bare.
Hidden in shadows, their essence flows,
Painting the world where no one goes.

In twilight's glow, secrets ignite,
Echoes of dreams take fragile flight.
They flicker and fade like the stars up high,
Leaving a trace in the wandering sigh.

Here in the silence, the heartbeats hum,
Radiant patterns, a silent drum.
Mysteries linger, weaving a thread,
Through time and silence, their stories spread.

In every glance, a luminescent spark,
A dance of the unseen, vibrant and stark.
With every heartbeat, the colors entwine,
In the realm of the lost, where we redefine.

Fragments of Reverie

In the corners of dusk, dreams take flight,
Whispers of laughter, fading from sight.
Pieces of memories, scattered like dust,
Gentle reminders of skies turned to rust.

Ripples of stillness, a moment in time,
Echoes of laughter, a soft, gentle chime.
Fragments of dreams woven in air,
Cascading colors in a world unaware.

Hints of a story, just out of reach,
Lessons in shadows that silence can teach.
With every heartbeat, more fragments appear,
A tapestry woven of joy and of fear.

In the journey of night, the stars softly gleam,
Hints of forgotten, lost in a dream.
Each fragment a whisper, each whisper a plea,
To hold onto moments, forever set free.

The Shrouded Sanctuary

Nestled in silence, a sanctuary waits,
Veils of the twilight, guarding the gates.
Shadows embrace, secrets held tight,
In the heart of stillness, a flicker of light.

Winds softly murmur, tales of the past,
Echoes of laughter, fading so fast.
A cradle of dreams, where wishes reside,
In the depths of the night, where fears often hide.

The dance of the leaves sings soft lullabies,
Invoking the magic that never truly dies.
Within this embrace, all sorrows unwind,
A refuge for wanderers, gentle and kind.

Here time stands still; the world is at peace,
A shrouded haven where heartaches cease.
In this sanctuary, we find our own way,
Guided by stars that beckon to stay.

The Lush Bastion

In the heart of the forest, verdant and deep,
Lies a bastion of life where the wild things leap.
Canopies whisper, secrets of green,
A realm untouched, where beauty is seen.

Under the branches, soft shadows caress,
Bright blossoms dance, nature's sweet dress.
Streams flow like laughter, pure and so free,
Carving a path through the roots of the tree.

In this lush haven, the world feels alive,
Every heartbeat a rhythm, every breath a thrive.
Birdsong and rustle meld into one,
A symphony played under the sun.

While time drips like honey from nature's embrace,
Peace and serenity find their true place.
The lush bastion beckons, a refuge so bright,
In the arms of the wild, we find our delight.

Chronicles of Seclusion

In quiet corners, whispers flow,
Secrets linger, shadows grow.
Time stands still in this embrace,
Finding solace in a hidden space.

Memories dance like fading light,
Cloaked in dreams, escaping night.
Pages turn in silence deep,
Where thoughts are treasures meant to keep.

Fleeting moments, a gentle sigh,
Chasing stars across the sky.
In this realm, the heart will soar,
A world untouched, forevermore.

Chronicles weave their silent song,
In solitude, we find where we belong.
Each line a thread, a story spun,
In seclusion, life has just begun.

Horizons of Hues

Morning blush paints the dawn,
Pastels spreading on the lawn.
Gold spills over fields of green,
Nature's canvas, fresh and keen.

In twilight's grasp, colors blend,
Crimson skies begin to mend.
Lavender whispers in the breeze,
Each hue a promise, pure at ease.

Stars unveil their silver tones,
Night's embrace, a cloak of stones.
Shades of darkness, deep and bold,
In this dream, new tales unfold.

Horizons open, wild and free,
A spectrum rich for all to see.
Every color tells a tale,
In this journey, we will sail.

The Hidden Tapestry

Within the threads of life, we weave,
Stories hidden, few believe.
Colors blend in intricate ways,
Mapping out our winding days.

Patterns dance in quiet grace,
Every stitch a sacred space.
Underneath, the secrets lie,
Silent truths that never die.

We gather pieces, lost and found,
In this loom, our hearts are bound.
Every tale a vibrant part,
Woven with the threads of heart.

The hidden tapestry unfolds,
Whispers shared, and love retold.
In every loop, a life entwined,
In this craft, our souls aligned.

Echo Chambers of Excitement

In echo chambers, voices blend,
Rising beats that never end.
Thrumming hearts and vibrant tones,
Cascading laughter, joyful moans.

Spinning stories, bright and clear,
Every shout a pulse we hear.
Resonating through the night,
In this space, we take flight.

Whispers of dreams ignite the spark,
Illuminating paths in dark.
Adventure calls, a thrilling ride,
In echo chambers, we abide.

Together we create the sound,
In this moment, joy is found.
Let the echoes fill the night,
In excitement, we unite.

Barriers of Beauty

In gardens where the roses grow,
Their petals soft, a gentle glow.
A fence of thorns, a secret way,
To keep the light from turning gray.

The river flows, a whispered song,
Beyond the banks, where dreams belong.
Yet shadows dance on edges steep,
As beauty's secrets softly sleep.

The mountains rise to touch the sky,
Their peaks adorned, a lullaby.
Yet storms may come and winds may tear,
But beauty lingers in the air.

In every heart, a silent plea,
To break the walls and learn to see.
For beauty thrives in hidden spots,
Where barriers fade, and love is not.

Luminous Enclaves

In corners bright where shadows flee,
A light that sparkles, wild and free.
Whispers of hope in quiet nooks,
Where dreams take shape like open books.

The sunlit glade, a secret sphere,
Where laughter builds and hearts draw near.
Embrace the dawn, the warmth it brings,
As joy takes flight on golden wings.

Through leafy boughs, a sunbeam streaks,
In tranquil hours, the spirit speaks.
These enclaves filled with warmth and grace,
Reflect the light of every face.

So seek the places, bright and real,
Where love and kindness softly heal.
In luminous enclaves, spirits thrive,
And in their warmth, we come alive.

Starlit Sanctuaries

Beneath the vast, celestial dome,
We find our hearts, a place called home.
In starlit sanctuaries, we dream,
Where wishes flow like silver streams.

The night unfolds with gentle flair,
A whispered wish, a quiet prayer.
Among the stars, our hopes take flight,
Guided by the softest light.

In moments still, where shadows play,
We find our courage, come what may.
Each canvas of the night inspires,
Infusing souls with endless fires.

So linger long in night's embrace,
In starlit sanctuaries, we trace.
A map of love in the dark sky,
Where every star will never die.

Mystical Boundaries

In twilight realms where magic weaves,
A tapestry of whispers and leaves.
Mystical boundaries softly hum,
With secrets old, they call us home.

The moonlight casts a silver spell,
In hidden paths, where stories dwell.
Through veils of time, the echoes sing,
Of ancient tales and timeless spring.

In forests deep, where shadows blend,
The boundaries blur, they twist and bend.
A magic touch, a fleeting glance,
In every heart, a timeless dance.

So wander where the spirits roam,
In mystical borders, we find our own.
For beauty lies between each line,
In realms where hearts and dreams entwine.

Echoes Beyond Barriers

In shadows deep where secrets lie,
Silent whispers weave and sigh.
Faint but clear, they drift and roam,
Echoes call, yet feel like home.

Across the void, their voices blend,
A harmony that knows no end.
Walls may rise, but hearts can see,
The song of souls that long to be.

Time stands still, a fleeting breath,
Capturing moments beyond death.
In every pause, a tale unfolds,
Of dreams once lost, now bright and bold.

Beneath the stars, a magic waits,
A bridge that spans our fates and states.
Listen close, let echoes find,
The love that bridges heart and mind.

Secrets in Stony Silence

In ancient stones, a tale confined,
Whispers linger, intertwined.
Each weathered face, a story tells,
Of joy, of pain, where silence dwells.

Yet beneath the weight of time,
Life pulsates, a hidden rhyme.
Cracks and crevices all reveal,
Secrets locked but ever real.

The stillness holds a quiet grace,
A breath of life in every space.
In muted tones, the past speaks clear,
To those who pause, who wish to hear.

In shadows cast by moonlit glow,
The stony silence starts to show.
Mysteries await the brave,
To touch the hearts of stones that save.

Enigmas Encased in Stone

Hidden truths in granite bed,
Sheltered whispers go unsaid.
Each layer tells of time's embrace,
Of earth's deep secrets, lost in space.

In every crack, a story sleeps,
While nature breathes and silence keeps.
Riddles wrapped in shadows bold,
Waiting for the brave to unfold.

Pathways forged through ancient rock,
Lead to places where time's clock
Ticks slowly, granting peace of mind,
To seek the answers left behind.

With every hand that touches stone,
History speaks, no longer alone.
For those who look with open eyes,
The enigmas found beneath the skies.

Whispers of the Enclosed

In quiet alcoves, secrets tread,
Where whispers linger, softly spread.
Curved walls cradle every sound,
In stillness deep, the lost are found.

Fragrant air wraps around the soul,
Encasing thoughts, making us whole.
Each sigh a promise, faithful, true,
Echoes of dreams we once pursued.

Within these bounds, a world unfolds,
Tales of the brave, the soft, the bold.
Beneath the surface, life does swell,
In whispered tones, all hearts compel.

The enclosed embrace holds time at bay,
While outside chaos fades away.
Listen close, let silence reign,
In sacred spaces, love remains.

Enclaves of Exploration

In hidden groves where whispers dwell,
Adventurers tread where few can tell.
Secrets bloom under the moon's soft gaze,
Paths unwound in a misty haze.

With maps unfurled and hearts aflame,
Each step a quest, none quite the same.
Mountains rise, and rivers flow,
A world unfolds, and spirits grow.

Through tangled vines and ancient stone,
Echoes call from ages flown.
The thrill of search, the thrill of find,
Unlocks the treasures in our mind.

In enclaves lost, where nature sings,
The joy of journey gives us wings.
Together we roam, forever bound,
In exploration, love is found.

Fabled Fortifications

Walls that whisper tales of old,
Where knights once stood, and legends bold.
Banners fluttering in the breeze,
Guard the dreams of memories.

Stone by stone, a fortress grew,
Through storms of time, it still holds true.
Within its grounds, the echoes ring,
Of battles fought and tales to sing.

Underneath the shadows cast,
The relics of a glorious past.
Candles flicker in the night,
Guiding souls with flickering light.

Each rampart holds a story dear,
Of love and loss, of hope and fear.
In fabled fortifications we stand,
Guardians of this enchanted land.

The Lattice of Dreams

Woven threads of night and day,
In the lattice where wishes play.
Glimmers dance in silver light,
Guiding hearts through realms of night.

A tapestry of stars unfolds,
Each one a wish, a story told.
We drift on whispers, soft and low,
To places only dreamers know.

Through corridors of endless thought,
The secrets of our hearts are sought.
In every shadow, every gleam,
Lives the pulse of a potent dream.

With open minds, we weave and spin,
Creating worlds where we begin.
In the lattice of dreams, vast and wide,
Every hope becomes a guide.

Chambers of Chimeras

In chambers deep, where shadows play,
Chimeras dance in bright array.
Creatures strange with forms that blend,
In a realm where boundaries bend.

Mirrors crack and secrets weave,
Glimpses hint at what we believe.
Dreams and fantasies intertwine,
A maze of thoughts, forever divine.

Through corridors of the bizarre,
We chase reflections from afar.
In this place where fates collide,
Every heartache finds a guide.

Chambers echo with laughter's song,
In this land, we all belong.
With each discovery, we embrace,
The beauty found in each face.

Dreams in Color

In twilight hues, where shadows dance,
A world awakens, lost in chance.
Whispers of wonder, in every shade,
A canvas of hope, in dreams displayed.

With every sigh, a story glows,
In vibrant tones, the magic flows.
Beneath the stars, our hearts take flight,
In dreams of color, we find our light.

A brush of fate, with strokes so brave,
Washing the silence of night's deep wave.
With every heartbeat, a new design,
In dreams of color, our souls align.

Through prisms bright, our visions soar,
In the realm of dreams, we seek for more.
Together we wander, hand in hand,
In this vivid world, forever we stand.

The Fortress of Fantasies

High upon the mountain steep,
A fortress stands, where secrets keep.
Walls of whispers, towers of light,
In the heart of dreams, a wondrous sight.

Guarded by stars, a mystic gate,
Inviting souls to brave their fate.
Within its halls, the stories weave,
A tapestry of hope, we believe.

In gardens lush, where echoes play,
The golden paths lead us away.
Through ancient doors, the magic binds,
In every corner, new worlds we find.

So come and wander, if you dare,
In the fortress strong, with joy to share.
For in these walls, our dreams ignite,
In the fortress of fantasies, take flight.

Echoes of Infinity

In the silence of the night's embrace,
Echoes whisper time and space.
Stars align with stories old,
In the depths of darkness, tales unfold.

Ripples dance on cosmic seas,
Carrying whispers on the breeze.
Every heartbeat, a timeless song,
In echoes of infinity, we belong.

Journeying through the vast unknown,
To realms of light, our spirits flown.
Each moment lingers, past and new,
In the echoes of infinity, we pursue.

So listen close, for in the air,
Are tales of love, joy, and despair.
In harmony, the cosmos sings,
In echoes of infinity, hope springs.

Whispers in the Air

Softly spoken on the breeze,
Whispers dance among the trees.
Carried lightly, thoughts inspire,
In the air, a gentle fire.

Tales of dreams and hopes untold,
In every sigh, a world unfolds.
Through sunlit days and starlit nights,
Whispers linger, sweet delights.

In the silence, secrets flow,
Carried high where wild winds blow.
Promises whispered, hearts laid bare,
In the stillness, love's soft prayer.

So pause a moment, take a breath,
In these whispers, find life's depth.
For in the air, we share our cares,
In the melody of whispers rare.

Elysian Environs

In gardens where the soft winds sigh,
Golden rays through leaves drift by.
Whispers of the ancient trees,
Breathe life into the gentle breeze.

Silent streams with laughter flow,
Beneath the skies, a vibrant glow.
Each petal paints a tale untold,
In hues of red and shades of gold.

Mountains rise with tranquil grace,
Embracing clouds as they lace.
In fields of dreams, our spirits soar,
To find the peace we all implore.

Elysian vibes, so pure, so true,
In every dawn, a world anew.
In nature's arms, we find our place,
A timeless song, a warm embrace.

The Embrace of Echoes

In caverns deep where shadows play,
Echoes dance and weave their way.
Whispers linger, filled with lore,
Each sound a key to distant shores.

Beneath the earth, the silence hums,
A secret place where truth becomes.
Voices lost, in time they fade,
Yet in the dark, their tunes are made.

Every call an age-old cry,
Stirring spirits held up high.
The air is thick with tales of yore,
Where each new echo seeks for more.

In the twilight's gentle hand,
We grasp the threads of a forgotten band.
In the embrace, a bond is found,
In echoes, hearts beat sound.

The Hidden Expanse

Behind the veil where shadows creep,
Lies a treasure, dreams to keep.
Paths of wonder layer the ground,
In the hidden, truth is found.

A world concealed from prying eyes,
Where secrets pulse beneath the skies.
Every corner, a story waits,
Unlocking time, it dictates fates.

In this space, the essence glows,
Fleeting moments, wisdom grows.
With every step, the heart expands,
In the hidden, we take our stands.

Winds of change through branches weave,
In the expanse, we dare believe.
Mysteries wrapped tight we roam,
Finding solace, we call it home.

Celestial Barriers

Stars align in a cosmic dance,
Painting skies with a twinkling glance.
Beyond the light, the shadows play,
Each constellation leads the way.

Galaxies swirl in silent night,
A symphony of pure delight.
Planets turn, their secrets spun,
In the echo of the morning sun.

Through the void, we seek our fate,
Past cosmic doors, we navigate.
Every heartbeat, a thread of light,
In celestial realms, we take flight.

Bound by dreams that touch the stars,
We journey far from earthly bars.
In the vastness, a truth we find,
Celestial barriers, love entwined.

Milton Keynes UK
Ingram Content Group UK Ltd.
UKHW022209221024
449899UK00006B/40